CAPTIVE IN AMERICA

A Gypsy Woman in Dixie

The Memoir of Merinda Soldano
With Sheridan Hill

Copyright 2014 Real Life Stories, LLC

All rights reserved. No part of this publication may be reproduced, stored in a retrieval system or transmitted in any form or by any means, digital, electronic, mechanical, photocopying or otherwise, without prior permission of the publisher.

This is a work of creative nonfiction, based in part on the life of Merinda Soldano. Dates have been generalized, and the names of most people and places mentioned herein have been changed in order to focus on Merinda, her journey, and her healing.

Library of Congress Control Number: 2014907557
ISBN: 978-0-9791355-3-8
Printed in the United States of America

Contents

1. LAMAR AVENUE — 1
2. JETTIE / MERINDA'S MOTHER — 10
3. I AM ROMANI — 13
4. SOLD AT THIRTEEN — 24
5. FROM BAD TO WORSE — 30
6. BESIMA / MERINDA'S FIRST CHILD — 41
7. RON / MERINDA'S HUSBAND — 46
8. FINDING JESUS — 52

1. LAMAR AVENUE

THIRTY OR FORTY MILES SOUTHEST OF MEMPHIS, YOU'LL FIND plenty of action. Head southwest, along the Mississippi, and you may be surprised to find the third largest gaming town in the United States: Tunica, Mississippi. Before 1990, Tunica was all over the news as the poorest place in America; now, people from the historically black town join other laborers with limited skills in casino jobs.

A few hundred years ago, the corridor between Memphis and Mississippi was called the Chickasaw Trail and only the brave or crazy followed it into the Chickasaw Nation. In the early 1900s, the city of Memphis paved the road and named it after Lucius Quintus Cincinnatus Lamar II, a politician and statesman from Mississippi who would no doubt be horrified by its present condition. Always an area of poverty, it has deteriorated since Elvis Presley and the blues greats played in these smoky clubs.

The new millennium found Lamar Avenue falling out of a landscaped neighborhood in Memphis. From there, it clunks along through the poor parts of town, grinds through warehouse country, and finally delivers itself into a few red dirt, one-legged towns in northern Mississippi.

Here, you can find everything a person with nothing needs,

mainly instant access to booze, cash, prostitutes, and mobile phones. Dirty storefronts and gritty parking lots offer pronto services that the poor need to bridge the gap between what slipped through their hands yesterday and what they're losing today: payday loans, self-storage units, title loans ("the cash you need when you need it").

One of the many pawnshops, Cash America, operates more than 900 stores in the U.S. and Mexico, serving "the under banked," as it calls them on its website. On Lamar Avenue, liquor stores will cash your government check so you can take the money you need for food and rent and immediately spend it on booze. The entire Lamar strip, with its dingy parade of stoplights, is a portrait of human pathos and urban ethnicity: O'Reilly Auto Parts, Lamar Jewelry and Pawn, New Hope of God Church in Christ, Soul Food and More, Cajun Chicken, Used Tires $20 and Up, Monument of Love Baptist Church ("the church that loves to love"), St. John Catholic Church, Homestyle Tacos, Boost Mobile.

A billboard for The Gun Exchange advertises handguns, rifles, and shotguns and stands proudly near the Welcome to Mississippi sign: that reminds us it is the "Birthplace of America's Music." The billboards draw a clear picture of who lives below them: Car Accident? Call 1-800-411-PAIN. We Help Injured Railroad Workers. Chasing Justice, Not Cars. Do You Have Syphilis? U.S. Marines: We Don't Accept Applications, only Commitments.

Finally, the urban poverty fades into hundreds of acres covered with tons of goods passing through Memphis on their way to somewhere else. Memphis is a virtual hub of commercial comings and goings along I–55, I–40, I–240, and I–69, as well as the Memphis International Airport and the railroad, all used by massive FedEx and UPS operations here.

It looks like half the goods traded, and returned, in the U.S. come through Memphis one way or another. The railroad yard for BNSF InterModal along Lamar Avenue is an otherworldly sight. A family of bright orange cranes tower 90 feet in the air, spaced along more than a mile of railroad track. Throughout the day and night, they move forty-foot containers, stacking thousands of them in tall columns. (Merinda's husband, Ron, helped construct the foundation for the cranes.) The containers get put on tractor-trailer rigs and driven across the county…and while the truck drivers are resting in between trips, they sometimes get lonely. Liquor stores are crouched near dance clubs ("Girls, Girls, Girls!"), and $29-a-night hotel rooms with plenty of parking for tractor-trailers.

On either side of Lamar Avenue, substandard housing abounds: houses that were ramshackle to begin with and have stood long in need of repair. There are several trailer parks, and it is here in Oakville trailer park that several groups of Memphis Gypsies have lived for more than 40 years. Another group lives in a trailer park off of Shelby Drive, which intersects with Lamar.

Merinda Soldano will tell you that she is "a traveler, a Rummeychul: the English Rummeychul." She pronounces it differently from how it is spelled: like too many of her people then and now, Merinda was pressured into dropping out of school as a pre-teen. Regardless of the lack of formal education, she is absolutely correct in referring to herself not as Gypsy but rather as Romanichal.

Romanichal refers to Romanian travellers who, since at least the fourteen hundreds, were chased out of some countries and fled from others when its natives tried to enslave them. In the United

States and Europe, we have erroneously called them "Gypsy," as a shortened version of "Egyptian": the place we thought they originated. For hundreds of years throughout Europe, laws have been passed to ban "the Egyptians," referring to the Romanichal.

It is hard to know which came first: the persecution of Gypsies (perhaps because they were not white, because they seemed mystical and were unknowns who moved around), or the stereotype of Gypsies as thieves, swindlers, and fortune-tellers who were always on the run from the law. Are they thieves or, as one encyclopedia notes, are they simply "resourceful…in leading a nomadic life in urban societies"?

They learned to keep to themselves and had specific terms for non-Romani people. Merinda and her mother pronounce it "gorger," and the word has a variety of spellings and pronunciations, among them gadze, gorgio, and gawja.

Merinda's mother, Jettie, offers a general idea of who the Memphis Gypsies are. "There's Gypsies that look like black people and call themselves Turks," she says, "then there's an Irish group and they talk a totally different language, and then there's Gypsies that have always spoken English, along with their own language, and that's who we are. A lot of the Gypsies have married out of their tribe. People who aren't Gypsies we call gorgers. I was friends with them all."

Language experts have verified that a fair number of words in the Romanichal language derive from Sanskrit, and indeed the Romani people can be traced to the Indian subcontinent as far back as the Eleventh Century. They share many traditional customs, including parent-arranged marriages ("thomnimata") for their daughters and specific rituals to honor the spirits of ancestors. Traditionally, when family members died, Romani would take their belongings, crush them, and use the remains to make the headstone.

At some point, the Romani left India and began to move through the Middle East, coming in contact with Muslims. (Part of the irony of Merinda's story—as well as an odd kind of throw-back to her roots—is that, although she lived in Memphis, Tennessee, she was married off at the age of thirteen to a young Arab man and lived in Memphis as a Muslim wife for the next sixteen years.)

The Romani are found in literature dating back centuries. William Shakespeare wrote of them in Antony and Cleopatra; a history of King Edward notes a Romani fortune-teller who pleased the Queen with his work. Romani sayings give some insight into the earthiness, faith, and sense of justice that runs through their culture, despite stereotypes of the opposite.

Te ala mangel o Del, vi dazi del puske ekh matora. (If God wished it, even a broomstick could shoot bullets.)

Patjival o manus an 'la vi anda gav xaljardo. (A righteous man will profit even in a poor town.)

Rrom corel khajnga, gadzo corel farma. (The Romani steals a chicken; the non-Romani steals the farm.)

The Romanichal are a world of paradox. Throughout history, they have been simultaneously the most free and the most persecuted people on earth. Before the 20th Century, many of them were nomadic, travelling in often-colorful wagons along dirt roads; therefore, they developed strict and complicated rules of hygiene. Men's garments were not to be washed with women's, clothing worn on the upper body, which is viewed as clean, was not to be washed with clothing worn on the lower body. In olden times, they washed their clothes and bodies in streams, and developed firm rules about who and what was washed upstream. Customs around women's clothing when they were menstruating also stipulated separate washing, downstream, but most references to the reasons for that seem to point primarily to a sense of menstrual blood as powerful, magical, and therefore respected as such.

"We have funny rules about cleanliness," Merinda volunteers. "For a long time, I would clean every bathroom every day, up and down, with Clorox. And my dad never would let another man use our bathroom. Ever, for as long as he lived." She will also vouch for Romani customs around using a woman's menstrual blood to have a desired effect on an individual, as she mentions in this book.

In the United States and in America, there is a rising interest in all things Romani, evidenced in popular books, television shows, in academic papers, and on a growing number of websites. Many, if not most, of them perpetuate the most negative stereotypes of what it means to be of Romani blood. Ian Hancock, who himself is a Romani as well as a Romanichal expert, works constantly to set the record straight. His books and online articles offer historical information that gives a more full picture of how these people have lived throughout the centuries.

According to Hancock's research:
- three Romanichal sailed with Columbus to the Caribbean on his third voyage,
- in the Seventeenth Century, Oliver Cromwell shipped Romanichals as slaves to American cotton plantations;
- freed black slaves in Jamaica and Cuba are documented as owning Romanichal slaves;
- in the 18th century, British Romanichal were deported to

Australia for its function as a penal colony.

In the fifteen hundreds, the English tried to assimilate English- and Welsh-born Romanies, offering them the possibility of becoming English subjects if they joined the general population. Three hundred years later, the English passed laws criminalizing the act of recreating, enclosing, or encroaching on a village green, aimed at running the Gypsies out of town. During World War II, the Nazis listed and exterminated hundreds of Romanichals. In 1960, caravans, a common form of Romani transportation, were formally outlawed from stopping together on English land without a license. A British Romani Council formed to fight for the rights of the Romanichals, and their freedom of movement was an issue as late as the 2005 elections in Great Britain. Restricted from public places, some Gypsies responded by buying land and creating their own communities.

Like Merinda, most of today's Romani are not full-blooded, having married other ethnicities for more than two thousand years. For this and other obvious reasons, the stereotype of Gypsies as dark-skinned is inaccurate. It is true that Merinda's natural hair color is jet black, but her skin color is as white as the average Anglo Southerner, especially combined with the bright, blonde hair she has worn for more than twenty years. When she praises Jesus from a chair in the Church of the Harvest in Olive Branch, or when she drives around Memphis, she would appear to be just another a white Southern Protestant. But when she pops in a convenience store and immediately spots the cashier as Arabic, she shocks him by speaking fluently to him in his native tongue.

Merinda's relatives are among what she estimates as several hundred people in the Memphis area who have Romanichal blood, and they have been here since at least the early nineteen hundreds. One of them, reportedly, was Elvis Presley, with his dark, good looks, soulfulness, and good boy/bad boy sex appeal. Other famous people with Romani blood include Charlie Chaplin, Rita Hayworth, and the poet known as Papusza: Bronislawa Wajs.

Both Merinda's grandmother and great-grandmother were fortune-tellers. Her mother, Jettie, recalls that before the city of Memphis would grant their business permits, the two women were asked to tell the fortunes of a dozen local business people, including lawyers. Their fortune-telling shop was in Southhaven, Mississippi, a suburb of Memphis. No reason you would know of Southhaven, but novelist John Grisham does: he practiced law for ten years there.

She is far from the average Tennessean. She is a Romanichal, a Southerner, and the ex-wife of a Memphis Arab. In post-911 America, Arabs and Arab-Americans play a growing part of everyday life and certainly business activity. There are several hundred Arab-Americans in Memphis, a Muslim Society, an Arab-American business association, and the University of Memphis offers Arabic language classes. One of the crown jewels of the city, St. Jude, is a heralded pediatric cancer hospital founded by an Arab-American, Amos Muzyad Yakhoob Kairouz. He was generally known as Danny Thomas. (Merinda's husband, Ron, helped construct an addition to St. Jude.)

Recently, Merinda "found Jesus." Coached by her husband, Ron Soldano, she puts her faith in Jesus. Both Merinda and her daughter tell stories of cruel emotional and physical abuse at the hands of her first husband. No matter how you look at it, Merinda has lived as a captive in the United States, home of the free. As a child, she was imprisoned by the oppressive conditions of her childhood, which she escaped only by becoming the thirteen-year-old wife of an abusive husband.

Could she have gotten loose, just walked out the door? Absolutely—if she had had a sense of wholeness about her worth as a woman and as a human being—but that critical perspective was missing. She has walked, and sometimes crawled, the painful, slow journey towards wholeness. Today, she says she leans more on God than on any man. Perhaps she has learned, as Henri Nouwen wrote in Our Greatest Gift, that "dependence on people often leads to slavery, but dependence on God leads to freedom."

2. JETTIE / MERINDA'S MOTHER

Jettie

MY MOTHER LIVED IN TENTS, BACK IN THE OLD DAYS. THE WOMEN fortune-tellers made most of the money in the family; their customers came to them. My mother didn't even know how to write her name, but she was a gifted fortune-teller. I wasn't gifted with it, but my mother and grandmother could tell you things that happened in the past, and things that would happen in the future. They had a place in Southaven. My grandmother went by Madame King, and my mother went by Madame Selena. They had to tell twelve people their fortunes—lawyers and business people—before they would give them their license.

I was born at Baptist Hospital up on Union. I only had six years of school and I'm not into the electronics, the computer. My nephew Clarence has looked up the whole Romani tribe. Most of the Irish Gypsies now live in the trailer park on Shelby Drive. I never mixed with too many of the Irish Gypsies.

Some of the men go away for weeks at a time and you don't know if they're stepping out on you or not. My father used to travel a lot for work, but he died when I was five years old of a massive heart attack.

Since I didn't have a father, we just stayed where we were. We were one of the homestead groups; we didn't move around.

Different kinds of Gypsies would come and camp in the trailer park where we lived. It must have been hard on my mom. She would go on the road with a man, and leave us kids without food sometimes. I had three brothers and they all married out of the tribe. They married gorgers. They worked like the Gypsies; they worked for themselves. Gypsies travel a lot, and their work takes them away all the time, sometimes the kids go with them. Now, a lot of them live in houses. Or they buy these campers and travel up and down with them, then sell them at the end of the year.

I stayed with my brother and his wife a lot when my mom was gone. Sometimes she took us with her and we stayed in a hotel. I didn't have supervision, but I had common sense. I knew what not to do. My mother died at 76.

Rummeychul love fancy bedspreads. We use a lot of Clorox, especially in bathrooms. We don't believe in letting visiting men using our bathrooms. And we don't want our kids to sit on a strange commode where somebody may have had a disease. It's a good belief.

We have very big funerals. After a funeral, the young ones get together and rent a place to dance together. They don't go to no clubs where white people would see their girls. They rent a separate place for parties.

When I started to have Merinda, my husband and my brother had gone to Pine Bluff, Arkansas. It was New Year's Eve, 1970, and they didn't come back until two or three in the morning. Then I went into labor after he went to sleep. He liked to drink, and he was a sound sleeper, especially when he had been drinking. I couldn't get him up. He just lay there and I was having labor pains. My mother was there, too. I got pissed off and went in the living room and sat down and said, "I'll just have it right here."

I was only about nineteen years old. My sister, Mary, came over about seven o'clock in the morning to pick up her kids; I would get them ready for school. She seen how I was hurting and she said, "Girl! You're fixing to have this baby." She got my husband up and told him, "Get in here!" So, he took me to St. Joseph's Hospital.

Merinda was turned the wrong way and they thought they were going to have to do a C-section but at the last minute, she turned. She weighed five pounds, four ounces.

3. I AM ROMANI

Merinda

IF I COULD GO BACK AND REDO MY LIFE, I PROBABLY WOULD HAVE told somebody what was happening at home so they could have helped me—even if they took me from my parents—instead of being a mom at fourteen. But I had never heard of such a thing as a social worker when all that started. I never knew there might be a way to get away.

Today, all I want to do is tell the truth about the things that have happened to me. I hope it will help other women. The only way I have lived through it is with God's help. Somehow, while there was nothing on the outside to verify it, I think I was believing in God without knowing it.

I was born on New Year's Eve, 1970, at Joseph's Hospital in Memphis. I am Romanichal; the English Gypsies. I am Romani. Being a Romani girl means you have to grow up fast and you have to make men like you at an early age. And you have to know how to cook and clean. I never had a childhood. My relatives would force us to put on short-shorts and wear makeup. My father's brothers tried to make me dance for them when we were at my grandma's house, and that's not all, either. I was only nine years old. I didn't understand what they wanted; I just knew it felt bad to me.

The Romani Gypsies have specific ways of dealing with everything. The old Romani people would go to the grave of their dead ancestors, talk to them, and ask questions about their future. Gypsies consider themselves "Travelers." That's what we call each other. Maybe that's because the words "Gypsy" and "Romani" have become synonymous with "thieves." In Europe, if you saw sticks in the ground with Indian cloths over them, that was the Romani houses. They walked everywhere, and when they came to town, they would beg for bread.

I don't speak Romani much but I understand Romani talk. I have leeway in both worlds: with the blonde hair, and I know both languages. My hair is jet black but I've been blonde so long it just blends in.

Those Gypsy TV shows and movies are all wrong. For one thing, the Romani people generally don't have big weddings. We have big funerals. Romanichal celebrate funerals and cry at weddings. They find their wives at funerals. It's always been that way, and even today, it is the same. When Ron first went with me to a Romani funeral, his mouth dropped open. He had never seen women dressed so sexy for a funeral: showing off their bodies in tight, short, dresses low-cut in the front.

For a funeral, the Romani dress up like they are going to a club, and they make even the little girls dress up and wear all this jewelry and makeup and prance around the funeral like they're in a beauty pageant so the boys will see them, and then ask the parents if they can have them. The younger the better, because there is such an emphasis on purity and marrying a girl who is pure, meaning that she is a virgin. Then, once she gets "stuck," as they call it, once she is no longer a virgin, the girl has to go. And usually they don't marry, they just run off. There are very few Romani weddings; that's why the TV show and the movie are a lie. I've never seen a Romani girl in a white dress.

You could go to our trailer park anytime and see the little girls in their shorts, makeup, and jewelry, prancing around so the boys can see them. You can look at my Gypsy friends' Facebook pages right now and see who just found her daughter a husband at a funeral. Their pages have Christian messages about Jesus all mixed in with the photographs of the girls in heavy makeup and pornographic expressions on their faces, and four-year-old girls wearing gold dresses and makeup. The parents name their kids after cities and states, sometimes the ones they were conceived in, and they give their daughters names like Princess Priscilla and Carnation and let them drop out of school.

Of course, the men wear gold medallions and have their shirts unbuttoned so you can see the gold piece on their chest. Gold pieces are sacred to Gypsies, and they all have certain rings they wear, like a gold lion's head. My sister's boyfriend got my father's gold ring; I didn't get nothing from his death.

We were sheltered. What I mean is, we weren't allowed to mix outside the Romani family. We lived in Oakville Trailer Park, where my mother's mother, Norma Jean, lived. She had six kids. There were five Romani trailers, all my relatives. We had the whole front part of the trailer park. Now there are still some Gypsies, but it is Mexican-dominated.

When I was eight years old, we moved from Oakville to Candlelight Trailer Park. Candlelight was surrounded by a chain link fence and there was a hill behind it. We found a hole in the fence and we would crawl through it out to Third Street and get donuts. We would save our change all week for donuts.

I went back to Candlelight not long ago and saw the tree that comforted me when I was sad or scared. I would run to it and cry on it. My sister and I would make our own fun, just walking around the trailer park singing songs from the band Alabama. Once my friend Barbara and I were trick-or-treating and we ran up some iron stairs that had a lot of spaces in them the way a fire escape does, and my shoestring got caught in one of those spaces. I fell down and hit my back on the bricks. I was running home with the other kids laughing at me and the whole time I was running, I was saying: I can't breathe! And they were all running behind me, saying: "You're breathing!" It seems like life has been like that a lot…me running around and just trying to get my breath.

There were also some Irish Gypsies there, and my mother used to tell us about the Irish Gypsies being thieves. I never stole nothing in my life. Sometimes we would take money from our parents to buy cigarettes, but that's all.

My grandmother went through five husbands. Some people said that she would sprinkle stuff on their food to kill them. I don't know about that, but they did all die before she did. Before she died, she gave me this little glass vial of powder and said: This will protect you. But I threw it away. She is buried in Pine Bluff, Arkansas, where most of our Gypsies are.

Nobody taught me about Jesus. My only knowledge of Jesus was when a bus would come though the trailer park and somebody would ask: Do you want to go to church? And my sister and I would sneak on it to see what it was all about. It was a Baptist church. That's all I ever knew about Jesus in my whole life. There was nobody to teach us. My mother was too obsessed with trying to chase my father down.

I don't want to make my mother look bad; she did the best she knew how. My grandmother used to leave my mom by herself while she went to clubs where she would sing while this man played music. When my mom was little, she would make breakfast for a crippled man in the trailer park, and that way she would earn money to go to school.

At seventeen, my mother was working at the Piccadilly and met a man; I'll just call him J.M. She says he raped her, and that is how my sister Julie came into the world. She was my mom's first child. But my mom was so young. She didn't know anything. She later found out he was married and had five kids from his wife. We also heard that he had sex with his daughters. One of those kids was born with watermelon head, water in his head, another was born with extra parts she didn't need.

Irish Gypsies marry their relatives. That's why they come out with little nubs. Sometimes Romani Gypsies do too, because one time my sister kissed a boy in the trailer park and when we went home I told my Mom, and she flipped out.

"Who?" she said, and when we repeated it she said, "That's your brother." But how are you supposed to know if they didn't tell you? After that, my sister started to rebel.

My mom's brother lived in Lakeview Trailer Park on 61. My mom's side of the Romani family is more like white people; my dad's side is straight Romanichal. My dad had been out drinking when my mom went into labor with me. She was in a chair going through labor pains with my sister watching, and my father finally came home and took her to the hospital. I was breach at first, and she prayed that I would turn around and be healthy, and at the last minute, I turned around.

My older sister was two years old when my mom married my father, Eddy. They called him Moe. He was born in Virginia. My father was an outcast because he had a different father from rest of the family. His father was an old, old, old Romani.

My dad's family was the type that all competed for who had most jewelry, makeup, clothes, cars, they had money. I had a lot of men relatives who made good money doing asphalt, painting, and repairs: the kinds of things Romanichal have always done. My dad had two brothers, John and Frank. John got shot in a fight when all the Gypsies surrounded a trailer where two women were fighting. My uncle was just standing in the doorway of his trailer when one of the women fired into the crowd, and it hit my uncle. He died eleven days later in the hospital. At the funeral, Uncle Frank laid on top of the coffin. That was his brother; he didn't want to let him go.

Gypsy boys would get a pickup truck at thirteen years old and start working at a young age in asphalt and construction-type jobs. Or they learned to live on the streets. My dad's parents took him out of school in third grade, but he could do numbers just like that, in his head.

The happiest and the funniest part of my childhood is when my dad would sing and play his guitar and my mom would sing with him. My dad would impersonate Elvis. He had the black hair and the tight pants and would move around and sing just like Elvis. Sometimes, I put on Elvis music just to remember my dad: *Suspicious Mind, In the Ghetto, Are You Lonely Tonight*. My dad would go out drinking and when he came home, my sister and I would be his deejays, playing records he wanted to hear and would sing to. He'd put on his Elvis suit and walk down the trailer saying: *Elvis has left the building*.

On holidays, we all went to see my Granny, Ammie, and she would fix food for us. She was a tough little woman. She had a big screened-in porch to keep the mosquitoes from eating us. She'd make us clean up the yard and rake it. My grandmother's house was so immaculate. She had us wash all her best dishes every morning with bleach.

She called the big room "the showroom." It had a long, dining room table and was full of antique Italian furniture. She would get so angry with us for going in there. There was a footstool, every few months it got fatter, and she would change the fabric on it. It turned out that she was padding it with layers of money and fabric. She had chandeliers that cost so much money. In fact, she could make those chandeliers shake just by wanting them to move. She would sit there for about fifteen minutes, and she would get the crystals on that chandelier to rattle. Some people call that black magic.

Granny owned horses. She would come and get me, stop at the Lucky Store Market and get us baloney and onions sandwiches on the way to feed the horses. She'd stop by K-mart and tell me, "Get what you want," she'd buy me outfits and shoes, but then I felt bad because she wouldn't do nothing for my sister because she wasn't blood-related. When Granny died, they took all of her stuff, crushed it, and made her headstone out of it. What's hers is hers.

I was a tomboy all my life. My sister Julie tried to take care of me. Me, Julie, and my cousin Samantha were a trailer pack. We had an initiation to get in our gang. We were ten years old. One time this boy, Charlie, started hitting me, he beat me up, and my sister said, "If you don't beat him up, I'm going to beat you up." So, I got in a fight with him. I bit his thumb and his ear, and then a friend of his jumped in on me.

My mom's sister, Aunt Daisy, had been cooking a big meal and was mad because we were late coming in. She brought us inside and pushed me up against the wall with a broom mashed at my neck. She held me against the wall like that, and I grabbed ahold of the broom to try to keep it off my neck. I guess she was afraid we were going to run back outside, I don't know. When she let me go, we sat down at the table and she fed us what she had cooked.

I really liked school. I didn't have a lot of friends, so I named my pencils: Sammy and Paul. Julie helped me with my homework, and I made straight As. I made all the honor rolls, got all the ribbons for citizenship and participation. Before they made me drop out of school, one of my friends showed me pictures of her prom, and that's all I wanted to do was go to the prom, be a model and a cheerleader. That's why I do what I do for my little girl now. I wasn't able to make those things happen for my oldest daughter, Bessie. My husband, Makim, wouldn't let her have friends or go to the prom. But I will make sure it happens for my little girl, Ella.

The first time we got to go dancing, I was twelve years old. The Gypsies rented a ballroom, and my sister and I went with Romani boys. My dad let us go with them because they were Romani. Sometimes, Romani parents will get their girls fake IDs so they can go to Romani parties.

I did get into trouble sometimes.

I remember when my sister Eddie was born, I was so jealous of her. She had a blue twirley chair. I got her chair spinning round and round and my mom took the chair and held me against the wall with it. I was upset, and I said she's the one you love, not me? My mom said, "No, I love you, too. But you gotta stop being mean to the baby."

My hair was long, and boys would pull my hair and play with it. I told this one boy to quit messing with my hair. Then I got up and hit him with a hairbrush. He started screaming and hit me, so I stuck him in the side with Sammy, my pencil.

They took me to the office. The principal, Miss Hoyt, wore her lipstick way up over her little lips to make them look fat.

I told her: "I didn't do it!

She says: What are you talking about? Who stabbed him?

I go: Sammy did it!

When she asked: Who's Sammy?

I had to tell her: My pencil!

She got the paddle and said, "Bend over," but I climbed to top of her bookcase. There wasn't much she could do until my mom got there, and then my mom got me down and paddled me.

On the last day of elementary school, we were on stage getting our awards. I was standing there with a friend of mine who was a mixed black and white girl, both of us holding our awards, but no one was there for us.

The next school for us was middle school, and the one I was assigned to had gangs. Four little girls got raped in the bathroom the first three weeks I was there. Finally, I talked my mother into taking me to Horn Lake Middle school, a really great school. It was a fifteen-minute drive from our trailer park down Highway 61 to the other school. I went for three weeks, but then Mom said she was tired of driving me so I had to drop out. I couldn't understand why they wouldn't let me finish school, because I made good grades.

After that, I would clean the trailer and wait for other kids to get out of school so I could play with them. By that point, none of the other Romani girls in our trailer park were in school, either. My mother would lay out in the sun on warm days and we would lay out with her. We would cook lunch and wait for other kids to get out of school. Since we weren't in school, we learned other things, like smoking cigarettes and hanging out with older kids who weren't in school. That's when my sister started smoking weed.

The manager of the trailer park had a son, and he had a crush on me. He did something to me. I was eleven years old. He held me down. I got pregnant. My mother drove me to the abortion, but I went in there alone. I wish my mom had at least held my hand. But her attitude was: This was your fault, and you better not tell your dad or you're gonna die.

If my dad had known, he would have asked my mom: How could this happen and where were you?

My sister was seeing the boy's brother, but my mother kept me in the trailer after that. That was the worst thing that ever happened to me. My mom set it up so that one of my cousins got some other boys and they beat him up unmerciful. His eyeballs were hanging out.

My dad would use the most vulgar language you could imagine to us. If we didn't have the house clean or something like that, he would say the worst thing anyone could possibly say to anyone. He called my sister bad names and told her she was going to become an American whore. She didn't deserve that.

My father drank twenty-four-seven and he cheated on Mom constantly. My mom waited every night for my dad to come home when he was out. She would have a rifle out for him, and he would have a knife. We saw this all the time.

My mom had a red Thunderbird with a white interior and she would go look for him. Sometimes she would take us with her. I remember ducking down in her car to hide from him. We would find him at the Airways Airport Hotel. With a toothless woman. I remember getting out and fighting a black man and the toothless woman when I was nine and my sister Julie was eleven. He must have been an employee there because he had a uniform. Mom was beating up Daddy while Julie and I beat up Ole Toothless for being with our Dad. How twisted.

One night my father bought my sister a Chevrolet Chevette and said we had to pay for it ourselves. I was twelve and Julie was fourteen. My mom changed our birthdates on our birth certificates so we could get jobs. I made $1.75 hour at the Hong Kong Chinese restaurant. I was just a kid. From then on, me and Julie were always together.

One time my sister, Julie, and I went to the coliseum for a wrestling match. Julie ran into a friend, and she gave him a ride home, so we were fifteen minutes late coming home. When she drove up to our trailer, my dad was sitting in front. As soon as we walked up, he came over and punched my sister in the head and then he began hitting me all around my ribs.

The next day, my sister called somebody from welfare, child services, and they came and talked to her. My mom went ballistic. She told them we were lying, and they went away, took my parents' word for it, and never came back. After that, my sister threatened them all the time that she was going to call child abuse, but she never called them again.

I just couldn't take it anymore. I had to find a way out.

As I relive that, my lifestyle then, it made me a better person: I know how not to treat my kids.

4. SOLD AT THIRTEEN

Merinda

ONE DAY, MY DAD BROUGHT A TURKISH WOMAN INSIDE OUR trailer. Then he looked at me and my sister and told us to go away. I remember looking at her and noticing that she wore a long dress and she was barefoot and she had crusty feet. When Julie and I came back, there was a huge old dude standing there—he looked like a big old cheeseburger—and my dad was talking to him about him taking me away. You could say he was arranging my marriage but I would call it selling me. I was only thirteen years old. It's a horrible feeling knowing that this is what you gotta do to live. I begged my dad: Please don't, please don't! I told him I would find somebody else.

I was working at Wendy's, and I had noticed this Arab guy that would come in the drive-through, in a different car every time. He always flirted with me and said things like: You're so beautiful; I just want to take you home with me.

So, the next time he drove through and said that, I answered him. I said: You gotta talk to my dad. I told him where we lived, and he came over. His name was Makim Jarrar. Sometimes he went by Tony. Later on, I found out he used alias names all the time.

Of course, my dad is a Romanian Gypsy so he was all up for it when Makim came over to talk to him. He said: If you want her, you can take her.

Right after that, my dad bought two new mustangs. That's why I say that he sold me; because there was no way he would have money for a new car, much less two new cars.

Makim took me to a hotel in New Jersey. He was eighteen years old and I was thirteen. I was so scared for him to touch me. I was just a baby. I had never had a period. I didn't have boobs. He didn't do anything for the first few days. Then, at the end of the week, he did. He forced himself on me. I didn't even know what was going on. He said: This is the way we do it. But I found out later that's not really the Muslim custom. The Muslim custom is for a man to introduce a woman to his family before he has sex with her.

Because of what he did, I ended up in the hospital.

We came back to Memphis and he told his mother about me, and we were married in his brother's house here. That's when my Muslim education began. For the wedding, his mother dressed me in the Arabic clothing for women, covering your head and your body. We were married in the spring of 1985 by a Muslim sheik. We didn't get an actual marriage license for years later.

We lived with his mother in her house, Rania Jarrar, for the first three years. All of a sudden, I had to learn how to be a Muslim wife: how to clean the way they clean, how to cook the way they cook. It was like being a Gypsy and a Muslim at the same time. She taught me the Muslim prayers, and I learned to pray to Allah. I'm a Christian now, but then I was only thirteen, and I didn't know any better.

Even though his mom was mean to me, I still love her for

teaching me to cook, because no one else had showed me anything in the kitchen. She only spoke Arabic, no English, so I didn't understand anything she was saying, and that made her mad. I had long black hair, and when she got mad at me, she would bite me on the arm or hit me or pull my hair all the way out. So, I started studying her hand gestures to figure out what she was trying to tell me, and that's how I began to learn Arabic. First, I figured out what they were saying and then eventually I figured out how to speak it back to them.

Makim started beating me when I was pregnant with Bessie. He had no feelings, no emotions. I went into labor with her in the fall of 1986. We were living with his mother, and I labored all night. I was only fourteen years old, so I didn't have any experience with anything like that but I kept telling him: I think its time, I think its time. But he wouldn't wake up.

I called my mother and she drove me to the hospital in her little green car we called "The Green Machine." I was in labor twenty-two hours and they had to use forceps because they said my body wasn't developed down there because I was only fourteen.

We named her Besima: it means, "smile." She has a beautiful smile. I thought she was a baby doll. I wanted to be sure she was always clean, and like I said before, Gypsies have funny rules about cleanliness, so I bathed her five times a day. I washed her so much that her skin got white and scaly. When I took her to the doctor, he told me I had depleted all her natural oils. She was the love of my life: I almost washed all the oil out of her bathing her so many times a day. I didn't use a car seat because I didn't have one, and no one had ever told me that was important.

Nobody taught me or my mother how to be a mom. We did the best we could. One time when I was driving with my mom and Bessie in the car, Bessie started crying. She was only about six months old, and she was wailing. My mother grabbed Bessie and held her out the window while I was driving, and said: I'll kill her! She's torturing you! She and her daddy are torturing you!

I said: Mama, she's a baby; she doesn't understand anything.

Even though he was a terrible husband, a terrible father, I feel that he loved me but he didn't know how to love. I don't think he ever got loved enough to know how to love. In the beginning of our relationship, I told my Gypsy granny that I thought I loved him and I wanted him to love me.

She said: Darlin, let me tell you what to do. When you have your period, get some of it and put it in his spaghetti. He will never stop thinking about you. And I did it.

He and I both had to grow up fast. His mother had brought him to this country when he was only thirteen. He didn't know any English. They stood on street corners in Chicago selling socks, hats, t-shirts, and scarves with his father. That's how he learned English and learned how to build a retail business.

Here in Memphis, at first his company was just a tent on a lot out towards the airport. They bought the land and set up a big tent. Inside the tent, everything was set up just like a mall: there were racks of clothes, shoes, hats, socks, bicycles. Later on, they got into selling cell phones and beepers and owning discount store chains.

He was nineteen years old when they got raided. That's when I found out that Makim and his brothers had warehouses where they kept sacks of money. This federal agent was hitting Makim so I jumped on his back, trying to help my husband. After they got Makim under control, the agent looked me in the face and said: Are you Arabic? He knew I didn't belong there with them and what they were doing.

I said: No, Sir. So, they let me go. That's when my husband went to jail for the first time. They kept him for three weeks. They said he was a potential threat to the United States. The FBI thought Makim and his brothers were shipping weapons to Palestine to kill Jews, and they watched them from then on out.

He used to do the worst stuff; he would have black people stealing computers, fax machines, and bring them to him to sell. This was the late 1980s, when cassette tapes were the thing, and he had figured out the market for bootleg music tapes and was selling thousands of them.

When a fire truck came to put out a fire on the street where his business was, he punched the fireman in the face and said, "Get out of the way; you're blocking my business."

Makim was making money hand over fist, legally, and illegally. One nice guy who sold things for Makim tried to tell me that he was dangerous. He said: You are so beautiful and so innocent; you should get out while you can. I never believed him. I thought I was in love. I was just a teenager; I didn't know anything.

He was a perfect provider; he would bring bags of money home, lock me in a room with it, and tell me: Count it. He would cut the carpet in the closet floor, lay packs of thousand dollar bills under there, and cover them back up with the carpet.

He would have me stack things and organize things in the store, but I wasn't allowed to just show up unannounced. If I forgot and drove over there, he would immediately beat me up. He beat my face into a wall. One time when Besima was with me, he beat a sink until it fell off the wall and pushed my face into the sink and pounded on the back of my head until my face was all bloody. Then he made me leave the building that way. I had to walk all the way through the store with a bloody face. Because I walked in without asking. A lady in the store saw me, stopped me, and said: Do you want me to take you to the shelter? I said: No. I was scared. I knew he would kill me.

Once when we were staying at a hotel out of town, I was in the swimming pool with my son and there was a skinny girl in the pool that my husband was noticing. She was nineteen years old. He brought me a drink, and he handed her a drink, and the next thing I knew, I woke up in the shower with water pouring in my face. He was in the bed having sex with the girl. She didn't know what was going on. The next day, she left a note on our door that she was so sorry about what happened and she wished she could take it back. He finally admitted that he had put something in my drink to make me "relax." That was our first vacation.

5. FROM BAD TO WORSE

It is probably hard for most people to understand why a woman stays with a man who beats her—even if he is her husband—but to young Merinda and women like her, it's all they know. From the time she was small, her father's beatings had raged over Merinda, her sister, and her mother; then her father committed the ultimate betrayal by trading her to an eighteen-year-old boy when she was barely thirteen. Makim was all she knew: his personality, his anger, and his desires, set the stage for the next sixteen years.

Merinda

I really wanted to finish school. For a while, I paid a person to take me to a class on Kirby Park road to get my GED. I would lie and pretend I was doing something else. I passed the math score with high grades but I never finished those classes.

When I got pregnant the second time, we lived in an apartment near Lamar. I was seventeen years old, and I treated Bessie like my best friend; we did everything together. She would help me clean the house, and she would walk with me as I cut the grass with the push mower. When our chores were done, I'd fill up her little pool, and we'd sit there and have lunch together.

In the summer of 1989, towards the end of my second pregnancy, my water broke but I didn't know I was supposed to go to the hospital. Then, one day when Bessie and I were napping, I felt the labor pains come on suddenly and very, very strong. I called Makim, but he just said: Call my sister. She lived nearby and could walk over, but by the time she got to the house; I was on the floor crawling in pain. I begged her to take me to the hospital but she said: Merinda, you know I can't drive! So, I put Bessie in the car and went myself. We named him Belal. At first, he was the ugliest thing because he looked so dried up. His daddy showed up three hours after he was born.

My third child, Jahad, was born blonde-headed in the spring of 1993. All I can say about his birth is that I had been a faithful wife to a very unfaithful and abusive husband for eight years.

In 1998, when I was in the hospital having my fourth child, Mujahed, I was bleeding to death. The doctor at St. Francis hospital told my husband that I needed a blood transfusion. Makim said: Muslims don't believe in that.

The doctor told him: She's going to die without it.

Makim said: Let her die.

So, the doctor gave me a shot of something to try to stop the bleeding, and later on, he told me that he had prayed for me. We called the baby Moomoo. Makim loved Moomoo. He even babysat him once or twice. When Moomoo messed his diaper, Makim didn't know what to do with it so he called me. I told him but he didn't understand. I had to laugh because when we got home, he had the diaper on but it was on backwards. Moomoo told people at church that he likes to be called Moses.

I didn't know what the word "abuse" meant. I was just living a life that was like a nightmare at times, and I really did not know how to make it any better. I had things, I had money, but I lived a dominated life. I couldn't see my family. I was told when and where to go, who I could talk to, who I could visit. I had no friends. When I turned seventeen, we had been married for four years, and I had five cars: a Ferrari, a Trans-Am, a huge Cadillac Escalade, and a Corvette.

From when I was thirteen until I turned twenty-nine, I got beat up, cheated on, spit on, pissed on. I was a maid for his family and a sex slave and punching bag for him. He done whatever he wanted to do with me. He slept with relatives of mine, in our own house. He abused my daughter's girlfriends when they came to visit. He would go out at night and have sex with different women, then they would call him and he would hide his phone and tell me not to ask questions if I knew what was good for me.

He threw me through a window. He tipped the refrigerator over on me. I've been dragged by his car twice. I have scars up and down one whole side of my body from being dragged by his car. I've had broken bones, a broken jaw. He tried to put his cigarette out by sticking it in my eye. The skin below my eye is still black from that burn. If I asked questions, he would beat me. I was afraid he would kill me if I ever spoke up.

If you have ever seen the movie The Burning Bed, that was my life. That was a really important movie to a lot of women because we saw our own lives there on the screen, and we realized that what was happening in our house was wrong. Sometimes, I would dream that a man in black was chasing me and was trying to put me in a box, and I would kick off the covers and tear at the metal blinds in the window while I was sleeping. I would cry out: Where is the help? Where is the help? I would wake up terrified with my heart pounding and my hands bleeding. I would walk outside, sit by the pool, and look at the stars and say: If there really is a God, get me out of here. If you're real, show me a way out of here; send someone to take me away.

I would find evidence of other women in his room. He had aliases. He had girlfriends who would come to the front door and ask for him under names I didn't know. Then I discovered that he had fathered a son before he married me. I had heard rumors that he had a black son, and he found me. He showed up on the doorstep at my apartment when he was seventeen years old. He didn't have to explain who he was, because he looks just like Makim. When I met that young man, I just took him right into the family. He calls me Mama to this day. I also recently found out that he had a daughter by another woman during our marriage. She is a young teenager; she found me and Bessie on Facebook.

He would stay out all night, and if I asked a question, he would beat me. He had his own table at the strip joints, paying those girls a thousand dollars a dance. Sometimes when he would come home late at night he would have a stripper outfit and make me put it on. "Let's see if you look as good as she did in it," he'd say. He bought one dancer a Corvette. I found it outside one time with makeup and women's clothing in it.

I did everything to be a good Arabic wife. I cooked for the azouma, the big dinner, when he would have fifty people over and they eat with their hands off large serving plates instead of forks and spoons and individual plates.

When his mother would come over, I had to wait on her hand, foot, and finger. When she walks into a room, you treat her like a queen: you take her coat, make her meal exactly the way she likes it, then her tea, then a fruit plate after the tea. The tea and fruit plate must be served after every single meal.

His mom used to tell me, one day he's going to marry an Arabic woman, he's going to get rid of you. All the time she would tell me that. But I don't believe in being mean to her even though she was a witch to me. I cleaned her house, I washed her clothes, I cooked for her—I felt that was my job—but I was the outsider. I do still care for the old woman; I am the first one who ever gave her a birthday present. I still take her a birthday present every year. She now says she is sorry she was ever mean to me, because I was so good to her.

I had to fix all these big meals for him and his family for the Muslim feast days. They never celebrated American or Christian holidays but I wanted to, so I would make big meals on Thanksgiving and Christmas. His family would come eat them, but most of the time, my family would stay away because of them.

I guess a person can only take so much. I think it all boiled up in me over time and I thought about getting revenge. I guess it made my dad mad, too, because one Thanksgiving he pulled one over on Makim's mother. My dad had been drinking, like always. He didn't wear a shirt; he thought he was so sexy with his jeans, bare chest, gold rings, and gold medallion. Makim's mother came in, wearing her Arabic head coverings. Arabic women are not supposed to let their body parts be seen by a man, and they can't let another man touch them. My dad knew this, but he was out for trouble, so he leaned in to hug her hello, and she started screaming in Arabic. He thought it was the most hilarious thing ever.

She sat down and we had Thanksgiving turkey and all the trimmings, but after dinner, he told me in Gypsy that he was going to take that thing off her head. When she got ready to leave, he gave me a signal—my mom and dad and I were all in the kitchen—and he goes out and tells her, "I gotta hug you bye, baby." She screamed so loud it hurt my ears, and she started biting her hand and heading for the door. But my dad reached out and got ahold of the end of her headscarf, and she just walked right out of it. Man, did she cuss! I can't repeat that here. Then my dad broke into his Elvis impersonation. My dad told that story for the rest of his life.

Arabs are not supposed to eat pork, either. For Thanksgiving, my dad would fix a bowl of hog jowls and put them in a bowl on the table like little pieces of bacon. Then he would sit down and play his guitar. One time he pointed out the hog jowls and told Makim to help himself to the food. He tasted them, and he ate every bit of it. I asked him: Do you know what you just ate? Khanaziir. He ran to the bathroom and threw up.

Sometimes I would feed him pork and beans and tear off the label on the can so he wouldn't see that I was feeding him pork. Gypsies love pork and beans. So did Makim. I did other things that I'm not proud of, but it was the Gypsy in me, I guess. After awhile, I got to where every time he hit me, I would pee in his tea.

I found myself getting revenge where I could, even when it meant I would be beaten later. I had already been beaten so much, it hardly mattered. At least I could get beating for doing something instead of doing nothing.

His brothers and sisters had seven or eight or nine kids apiece, and no respect for anyone. Their kids were running all over my house and tearing it down and I wasn't supposed to say anything. I was just supposed to clean it up when they left. I was the American sharmota, they called me: that means bitch, or whore.

They all loved this chocolate cake that I would bake, and one year I thought: If they're going to ruin my Christmas, I'm going to ruin theirs. When I was making the cake I put in dozens of crushed Exlax pills, and they all shit their pants before they left. Every one of them. And I loved it. That was in 1992, and it still gives me a good laugh to think about it. But he did beat me because of that.

In 1993, Makim had to turn himself in because he had learned about all the evidence they had on him. He looked at me and said: You're going to be faithful aren't you?

I said: yes, you're all I know.

He had already told me several times before: If you ever leave me, I'll make you crawl on the ground like a snake.

He was sent to eighteen months in the federal prison on Navy Road, a minimum-security facility. There is a chain link fence that separates the prison grounds from a neighborhood there in Millington, Tennessee. That's where inmates go to meet people, have sex, and just walk out. So all he had to do was walk through the woods and come right through the fence.

The kids and I visited him every weekend at the facility on Navy Road. Jahad was five months old. He made me wear the Arabic scarf over my head.

One day when I visited him in jail, he said: I wish I could put you in a box and just give you water and a piece of bread every day. Instantly, I remembered that terrible nightmare where a man in black was chasing me, and I knew it was him. The bad man in black was my husband.

Even when he was in prison, I would do everything he

said: meet in the woods and bring cigarettes and food and new jogging suit; have sex with him; drive him to a taco place. During Ramadan especially, he would make me put food under there and have sex with him. I am embarrassed about that now, but at the time, I didn't know who Jesus was. I was afraid of him, even when he was in prison. All he had to do was make a phone call and I would be dead.

When Makim got out of jail, he went back to doing everything he had been doing before. The abuse got worse the longer we were married. And most of the time when he beat me, he would have presents for me. He busted up my kneecap and then brought me presents and lay on the bed beside me while I was lying there in pain.

Makim's father had abused him. He would tell his sons: Bring me my cigarettes. But he had already told them not to ever touch his cigarettes. So, when they brought him the cigarettes, he punched them in the face. Makim's father would say things like: You're nothing. You're a piece of shit.

In the summer, he liked to go to Las Vegas, see the shows, and gamble. Sometimes he would take me, and one time he gave me a thousand dollars to play with. I sat down at a blackjack table with all these boys. We were all pretty new at it, but Makim had showed me how to bet and I showed this guy, Matt, how to bet. When he won, he put his hand on my back as a way of saying thanks. It was very innocent. But Makim happened to see it. He came over, escorted me upstairs, and broke my arm. Then he wouldn't let me go to the doctor for the next two days. After we went home, I did go to the doctor. I lied and said I fell down the stairs.

My second son, Belal, played soccer. Every time I took him

to a game, I had a black eye or a bruise on me somewhere. A lady used to say: I know he's hitting you. People would look at me and say: I'm gonna call the police. I would say: No, I'm okay. The door hit me in the face.

I went to every soccer practice and every game. Once, when I took the kids out of town for a soccer tournament, I came back and all of our family pictures had been taken off the walls and from every dresser in every bedroom. But someone had messed up the bed in my daughter's bedroom. Bessie used to love Justin Timberlake, and she had his posters all over bedroom walls. I found out that Makim had taken a stripper to Las Vegas and then brought her into our house while I was gone. When I confronted him, he pulled the refrigerator over on top of me. A few days later, a friend of mine found out who it was and where she lived.

I knocked on the door, and when she opened it, she was wearing a sapphire necklace and ring that I knew he must have given her. I asked her if she just returned from a trip to Las Vegas with an Arab man, and she said: Yes.

Get in my car, I told her.

She said: Are you going to kill me?

No, I just want to show you something.

When we got to my house, she said: Isn't this his brother's house? There's a room with Justin Timberlake posters in it.

No, I told her, it's our house. I took her to Bessie's bedroom, which she recognized, and when I told her it was his daughter's room, she started throwing up.

It was a life of deceit and secrecy, even though we had everything that money could buy. When the kids got older, they called him "The bank." That's how they knew him. They never called him "Dad." Shopping was my only peace of mind. I had beautiful clothes and jewelry. I had a new car but he would beat me if I went some place that he didn't approve of ahead of time.

It was a life of abuse and domination, especially for Bessie and me. I tried to never tell her what was going on, but she knew because she saw how he abused both of us and controlled both of us. Makim would never let her have friends.

I once took her to a skating rink and went to a pancake restaurant to wait while she skated. I didn't want anyone to see our car there, and I didn't want her to feel like she was being watched. But Makim had hidden a microphone in the sun visor, and he heard me call a friend of mine and ask him to please take care of Bessie.

Makim called me on the phone and said, "You're making my daughter a sharmota, just like you."

I said, "I'm letting her have a life."

He said, "She's not going to have an American life."

He molested several of Bessie's girlfriends. When I was pregnant with Moomoo, he would corner one girl somewhere in the house and order her to do things. She was just a young teenager. She had never been confronted with anything like him, and he was very forceful. He was very threatening. You knew that he could and would hurt you if you didn't do what he said. One day, when two of Bessie's girlfriends were out shopping with us, one of them said, "Susan has something to tell you." That's when I found out. So, she told me that Makim had offered her money. Another friend came down the living room stairs screaming and described how he had attacked her sexually. Another one he tied up in the laundry room and started molesting her.

When Bessie learned about the abuse, Makim bought her a flower and a ring and told her he was sorry. She was eleven. She was destroyed from that day on. She understood what kind of man her father was, and that is just too much for a young girl to have to bear.

6. BESIMA / MERINDA'S FIRST CHILD

Besima sits at her mother's kitchen table. The blood of her ancestors—Romani, Arabic, Indian—curses through her veins. It is a potion of persecution, survival, and resurrection. Her composure is palpable, and odd when juxtaposed against the torrential abuse she has known in her short life. Anyone looking at her will be struck with the beauty and the innocence of this young woman who has endured so much. Her sleek, black hair is a sheath down her back, and around her face, it frames the perfectly applied dramatic eye makeup of an Indian woman. The expression in Besima's large, black eyes is a mixture of pain and knowing. "My mother did the best she could."

Henri Nouwen has said, "Compassion requires us to be weak with the weak, vulnerable with the vulnerable, and powerless with the powerless." By anyone's markers, an authentic experience of compassion moves over Bessie's face when she speaks of the extreme difficulties her mother has endured. But it is for Besima that we also must cry. The abuse that besieged Besima and her mother from her father's hands is hard to fathom. She was beaten in utero, then as an infant, then as a youngster. Besima suffered the trauma of helplessly witnessing her father beat her mother on a regular basis, year after year. On a trip to the grocery store, her mother left her sleeping in the back seat of the car with her father in the front seat. When Bessie work up to find her mother gone and began to cry, her father smacked her face. Merinda returned with groceries to find her three-year-old screaming uncontrollably as a red handprint appeared across her small cheek. Besima's access to the world outside their home was severely restricted, and when as a young girl she invited girlfriends over to the house, her father sexually molested them. As is the custom in some Romanichal and Arabic families, he married off his daughter when she was a teenager, too young to decide for herself who she might want to marry. It shouldn't be surprising that teenaged Besima ended up with a man who physically abused her. But her groom and his family were important to her father's family business.

"I don't see how my mom gets up and goes on every day," Besima says, as tears begin to stream down her face. "She has been through so much. Her entire world revolved around us when I was little, and despite being beaten by my dad, she tried to protect us and take care of us the best she could. I think the first time my mom experienced freedom was when my dad went to jail for the first time. Then she took us to baseball games and everyday things that most people do, and she was so happy. She had a real smile. She felt free, and she didn't have to lie about where she was going."

Bessie

I don't speak Arabic, but I understand it. I learned it from going to Palestine a few times: once when my dad took me and my mom, and when his mom took me. He said he wanted to show us what it was like in his country, and his father's compound and lemon trees and other fruit trees. My mom and I stayed in the house most of the time there, because women were only allowed to go out on Thursdays. If we did go out, he made sure we wore the shaylah to cover our faces. It was strange because you were constantly reminded of the hatred there between the Israelis and the Palestinians. Four days out of the week, the Israelis would cut their water off and they couldn't flush a toilet or wash themselves. When Makim took us to a water slide in Israel, he made us take off the shaylah so the Israelis wouldn't throw rocks at us.

Arabic people and Romani people both marry their daughters off young, and when you marry a man, you are marrying his entire family. In both cultures, money means a lot; it's all about having material things and showing it off. The way they treat their women is the same: if you're a woman, you're below the men: you should stay home, not work, and you should leave the room when other men come in the room. The only real difference to me is that being Romani you can dress however you like, but Arabic women must dress conservatively.

My grandmother and grandfather weren't rich Gypsies. My grandpa wasn't into material things like other Romani men. When my mom met my dad, they were crazy about him because he was Arabic and he was going to make a lot of money.

I was always on my mom's side because I did see everything my dad done to her. She was a child when he started doing those things. I begged my mom to leave him but she said we would have a hard time if we did.

When my mom and dad were about to divorce, I was fourteen, so my dad got me engaged to an Arabic guy. He didn't want me to go with my mom and he didn't want me to be near Ron. He took me to Palestine and finally when I got to come back, I chose to live with my mom.

Being the daughter of a teenage mother, I was more like a friend to my mom than anything. We were best friends. I was also good friends with my mom's sister, Anne, and I have wonderful memories of staying with my grandmother in the trailer park and playing with my mom's sister there and at my house. Anne could come play Barbie with me, swim in our pool, and jump on the trampoline. She was one of my only friends. I was not allowed to have guy friends. In sixth grade, I made friends with a guy named Robert, and I also met a girl named Carol and we were all three friends. She was one of the first people who came out and told me what my dad had done to her.

Social workers came to the school and investigated, but my dad would tell me: She's lying; her mom's a lesbian and it's her fault. He tried to blame it on her. My friends who had been abused didn't want to have to go through making it public, so they wouldn't press charges.

My dad didn't tell me I couldn't go to school, but he had gone to jail and he was arranging this marriage for me, so that was the end of me being in school. He wanted me to marry my first cousin, his sister's son, and I didn't want to do that. I told my dad: Since this is going to have to happen, I want a part in the decision. The guy I married was engaged to someone else at the time, and my dad spoke to their family and he broke it off and married me. I had my twins with him.

For a long time I hated my dad, I really did. I think the closest I ever felt to him is when he was in jail and I was married. He was only out of jail for about two months before they took him and deported him. I used to beg my mom to leave my dad because of how bad he treated her. I think my mom tried many times to leave my dad and go back home, but my grandmother would tell her she needed to put up with it if she wanted her daughter to have a good life. So, my mom never felt that she could go back home.

Now, I just hope that my sons grow up to be men who don't abuse the women in their lives, because they have seen things they shouldn't have had to see. But like my mom, I try every day to do better, to give them something better. You cannot change what happened in the past, but you can try to do better right now.

7. RON SOLDANO / MERINDA'S HUSBAND

NESTLED IN THE DENIM OUTSKIRTS OF THE SMALL TOWN OF OLIVE Olive Branch, Mississippi, is a modest home full of heart and surrounded by handmade signs that Ron Soldano put together from scraps of metal and wood. On them, he paints messages of love and Christian faith. Like Merinda, Ron is blessed with above average looks. In fact, his Italian good looks landed him a few gigs as a print model and a television show appearance. Also like Merinda, his life hasn't been the stuff of fairy tales. Some of his choices as a younger man were nothing to brag about. But he found a way to pull himself up: he discovered a well that quenches the thirst of human desire, and he drinks from it every day to stay strong.

Jutting out from the flatlands surrounding Highway 302 in Olive Branch, Mississippi, the large, Church of the Harvest building stands a few miles from Ron and Merinda's house. For more than a decade, Ron has served at Church of the Harvest as an usher, small group leader, kids camp counselor and now as usher captain. He began bringing Merinda here before they married, and the church has stepped forth many times help the couple through tough times.

Banners on the sanctuary walls remind congregants to love God, love people, and serve the world. Following the contemporary

Christian movement, the organ has been hauled off along with the grey-haired organist, replaced by hip, young men sporting electric guitars and full drum sets, unafraid to make a loud noise. Lyrics for the songs are projected onto the wall behind the stage.

On a cold January Sunday, ushers and greeters hand out notes Pastor Bob Thomas has prepared to accompany his message. He reminds them where to find the online source for today's talk, and some people are checking their smart phones or digital pads. The scriptures and notes are also projected onto the tall wall behind Pastor Bob. A few congregants still bring their Bibles. Today, Thomas focuses on the upcoming twenty-one day fast. He offers health tips and provides a handout of resources, along with a recipe for what health food followers have long called "the master cleanse."

"Fasting moves us to receive God's grace," Thomas says. "Fasting helps you to submit to God," he says. "You know the part of you that doesn't want to fast? That's the part of you that needs to fast."

Ron

THE CHURCH OF THE HARVEST, AND THE THOMAS AND STEWARD families, have played a big part in saving me, and I am so grateful to them. Church of the Harvest is a nondenominational, spirit-filled congregation made up of believers called to carry a good news gospel of God's amazing grace. We are passionate about modeling an abundant Christian life based on the finished work of the cross. The church believes every member is called to be a minister in their sphere of influence.

I was raised in a Christian church. I knew Jesus, but I had chosen the wrong path in my youth. I had gotten involved in drugs when I worked in construction. At the same time, I knew something in me was changing. I knew I didn't want to be on that path. The last straw was when I had taped about five ounces of methamphetamine against my leg. Walking through the Salt Lake City airport, I felt it break loose. With my next step, I felt it roll down my pants and out in front of me. I am pretty sure the security person saw it. But I picked it up, put it in my pocket, and as I walked away, I thought: God, if I get through this, I'll never deal with drugs or do them again. You know something? That guard did not turn me in. And I did start to go clean then.

I lived with two brothers, Brad and James, and their dad, Dave. I worked for the family. Mike S. was a devout Christian and told us the only way we could get our paycheck is to come to church on a Saturday night. Brad took me to the Church of the Harvest, and when I heard the preacher do the altar call, I knew it was time. I went down the aisle and gave my life back to Christ. I felt that I was leaving a dark road behind me.

Driving home, Brad decided to go to the bar.

I said: Dude, we just left church! But he insisted that we were going, and he was driving, so that's where we went. I wasn't planning on drinking but he bought me a beer, and I sat at a barstool holding it while he went up to these two girls and asked one of them for a light.

Merinda turned around and looked at me, and she was so amazingly beautiful, I was just stunned. I smiled this big cheesy grin. Then she just ran. What Merinda's ancestors called fortune telling are called gifts of the spirit in the Bible. Merinda has those gifts, so her spirit knew exactly who I was, because the butterflies hit her stomach so bad she was sick to her stomach.

I waited around, watching for her, and when she came back, I asked her if she would save me a dance. After awhile, she went over to the side of the dance floor where they played slower music. I was waiting for her, to get the chance to dance with her.

When we were dancing and I was holding her, I could not stop staring at her face. It must have been awkward for her because I was just staring at how beautiful she was. Finally, we kissed. Then she took me to the side and said: I have four kids.

I just said: That's cool.

I have a three-day rule where I don't call a girl for three days. She called me several times but I didn't call her. So then she left a message like: Nice to meet you; never mind. So, I called back. After that, we were just all over each other. Anytime we could be together, we were. I was in awe of her. I felt like I was in a movie. Here was this beautiful girl in this beautiful car. She'd bring me lunch and write me notes, drive by in these rich cars, and I was just a rod buster with work tools hanging off my body. She came to my work with thousands of dollars in the car, as much as fourteen thousand dollars, saying: You can have it if you want. I never took any, but I may have regretted that a time or two.

I don't know where she learned to drive, but she could drive fast around city streets, and nobody could ever catch her. She was like a stunt driver in the movies. When we had only known each other for a few weeks, Merinda picked me up to go out to dinner and we noticed someone following her. We were headed from Coldwater to Southhaven in her Cadillac, and this car starts getting closer. Merinda sped up to a hundred miles an hour, and still the car was there. Then she gets up to 135 miles an hour. Three Southaven police cars start following us, two more join them, and she pulls off into a Southaven Walmart with three cop cars right behind us. The other two kept going, trying to catch the other car.

As she was stopping the car in that parking lot, we looked at each other and I felt an adrenalin rush. Not from driving, I always drove fast. It was from being with her. It was a reaction between us, the excitement of being together. This was before the police wouldn't let you get out of your car, and Merinda just got out of the car, walked back there, and did her thing. She always got out of tickets.

We figured those guys had been hired by Makim. Any normal person would say: Why would you want to be with a woman who has people trying to kill you because you are with her? But everything in me said: Dive in feet first; yeah, this is my girl now.

Makim tried everything to pry us apart. Makim offered me money to stay away from Merinda. He offered me a hundred thousand dollars if I never came back. When I said no to that, he said: What if you moved in with us?

One time, some guys were sitting outside my house with guns pointed at the house. I didn't see them but my roommate, Dave, did. I didn't think Dave had never been in military service, but he had an artificial leg and he would walk around the house wearing combat gear and wielding guns. He'd have a shotgun plus a rifle on his back, and two handguns tucked in his pants. He loved guns. When he saw those guys out front, he busted out of our front door and came running out of the house in full combat gear, but then his leg fell off while he was running down the steps. You had to admit that was pretty funny.

When the tragedy of 9-11 happened, Dave tromped down to the basement steps where I rented a room. He was wearing a tactical vest with grenades and shotgun shells tucked in different places. He was wearing a helmet with a dent in it. He had told me that he got hit with a cannon in combat. He pointed his shotgun at me and Merinda and said: We're under attack! All foreigners are getting deported, so get your asses out of my house!

I didn't know what had happened or how serious the situation was.

Makim had me arrested for allegedly trying to kill him. I drove a 1990 twin turbo Nissan 300ZX; not a car you see every day. Makim found a car just like mine, and had a guy come to his house in the 300ZX and shoot up his house. Of course, his neighbors saw the car, and Makim went down to the police department and signed an affidavit saying I had shot up his house. So next thing I knew, I had an attempted murder charge on me. But as it turned out, when his house was shot up, my car was sitting in a garage in Mississippi with a blown head gasket. I turned myself in and hoped for the best. They drove all the way out there to see if I was telling the truth, and then I was cleared of the charges.

8. FINDING JESUS

FINALLY ACKNOWLEDGING THAT SIXTEEN YEARS OF HER HUSBAND'S unfaithfulness, betrayal, and beatings had destroyed their marriage, Merinda found herself willing to go out with friends. A chance meeting with Ron sparked instant love-struck confusion for them both. They were able to date because Makim was either in jail or preoccupied with one or more women he orbited around. When Makim found out Merinda was seeing someone, he reacted with violent threats.

In the early months of their relationship, Merinda was afraid Ron was not serious about treating her right, and wrote him a letter two days after Valentine's Day, 2001.

"I want you to succeed with your calling. I want to be the woman standing behind you. This is our chance to make a difference in ourselves and others. We bonded inside; we've both been through so much in our lives, but we keep trying. You can be my strength, and I know I'm your motivation."

In time, Makim was deported to his native country. Ruefully, Merinda notes that Makim's deportation to the Middle East allowed him not only to start anew, but also to conveniently avoid the kind of financial responsibility that would normally be expected from the main breadwinner at the end of a sixteen-year marriage involving four children. She says authorities informed her that the reason they could not prosecute him for lack of child support is because he lived in another country. He can be found on a social media website, pictured with his young Middle Eastern wife and his children by her…just as his mother often predicted to Merinda.

Merinda

WHEN I MET RON, IT WAS THE BEST YEAR OF MY LIFE. I NEVER had the freedom to do anything before that. Makim had found this Lebanese girl and brought her down here from New York. He got her an apartment on our street and bought her a car, and he started leaving me alone. So, when my neighbors, Mark and Terri, invited me to come to a club with them, I got very excited and very scared at the same time. It was February 18, 2000. I had never been to a club before. I had no idea what to wear, so Bessie picked out my clothes.

When we got there, I stayed in the car and cried, and cried. Terri finally came out and said: If you don't come in, we are leaving. So, I went in and stood by the dance floor.

This guy came up to me and asked for a light. Then he said: Do you like country music? I looked past him at this young man behind him. He was wearing a cheesy smile and a blue collared shirt and khaki pants and he had his leg cocked up on a chair. He was gorgeous. The butterflies hit my stomach so fast that I ran to the bathroom and threw up.

When I finally composed myself, I came out of the bathroom and he was waiting for me. He asked me: "Will you save me a dance?" Of course, I said yes.

When we danced, he would not stop staring in my face. I just stared back at him. Then he just kissed me and my skin melted. It felt like my soul was electrocuted. I just wanted to faint.

We started to see each other regularly. Part of me knew that Makim would get revenge on me and part of me didn't care. Even though Makim had other women that he saw all the time, he had me followed regularly. Ron left messages on my phone, and Makim found them. When Makim found the messages, he had me arrested. He scratched up his own neck, called the police, and told them I did it. When they arrested me and I told the policewoman how he abused me, she said: You have acrylic fingernails, and you're telling me you can't get away from him?

The next day, I got out on my own recognizance. The judge knew what I was going back to, and he said: When you go home, don't speak to him.

When I got home, I was so hungry. I went into the kitchen to make a sandwich and Makim walked in. He said: I found your boyfriend, and I'm going to have him killed.

Ron was only 24 years old. He had never been married; he had never had kids. I'm five years older than he is, and I was afraid for him. I had spent the night in jail, I was just out of sorts, and I said: Leave him alone. If you touch him, I'll kill you.

But Makim had a recorder running in his coat pocket, and he took the recording to the police and they arrested me again. They put me in jail that night, but the next day I had court and they released me. But I had nowhere to go at that point. Ron was living in Coldwater, Mississippi, and when I called him, he said: You can come here.

While I stayed with Ron, Makim's brother's wife took my children so I could figure out what to do.

Makim had us followed constantly. He had men come by Ron's house waving guns from their car. He had men shoot up his own house from a car just like Ron's, and then had Ron arrested for attempted murder. I had more jewelry than Brittany Spears, a lot of it handmade with beautiful Arabic jewels, but I pawned it to get Ron out of jail. He was proven innocent because his car had blown a head gasket three days prior and it was in a shop in Senatobia, Mississippi.

Makim told Bessie that I had cheated on him. It was a difficult time, but I felt that my future was with Ron. I felt that my life could change for the better with Ron. He was the answer to my prayers. Not only was he good to me, but he took me to church. It was the first time I had been in a church, not counting as a child a few times for Bible school. Ron introduced me to the Lord, and I know he will get credit for that in heaven. I was shivering when he first took me. I had the jitters so bad; it was like having the chills. My heart was pounding. I felt the Holy Spirit in my body.

When my divorce came through, he was ordered to pay me seven hundred dollars a month in alimony. Makim was in jail, but his brother would meet me and give it to me. One day after meeting with him, I put my purse on top of my car and drove off. When I realized what I had done, I stopped but my purse had flown away with the money in it.

I had thirty dollars in my pocket. I told the kids: I guess that's gonna have to last us the whole month. The next day, I said: God, I really want to go to church today so please help me. My kids weren't used to getting up to go anywhere on a Sunday, so it took a lot of effort. We all wore yellow. Everybody stared at us; we were so pretty. We sat down in the pew and I told Bessie: I have to give money today. Ron had taught me that was what you should do: give money in church. I took the envelope and my daughter looked at me and said: Mom, what are we gonna do for lunch?

I said: We're gonna try this.

I put twenty dollars in the envelope; I kept ten for myself.

Then I felt a tapping on my shoulder. It was a man with a long beard, and he said: It's good to see a mother teaching her children to give; take this gift. And he handed me five twenties. I gave twenty and he gave me five twenties back. It was just as Ron said: God will work miracles.

Later, I asked the pastor about it. I described the man, but the pastor said: I've never seen anyone like that in here. I repeated it; what he looked like. But the pastor said: I think you have an angel. That same angel returned in my life seven years later when I was in great need. A woman at work accused me—in front of everyone—of stealing her check. I didn't know anything about her missing check, and I told her so. Then she needed a ride home, and I gave it to her. I had just gotten paid, and I put my server book on top of the car and drove off. Nobody could find it. I was destitute, and that was our food money.

Five days later, they told me at work that someone was waiting to see me. I went outside, and there was the same man. His beard was different, but I could not forget his eyes. He handed me my server book with all of my cash and my check. He also added five twenties with a note: Now I help you again.

I don't know how he found me because my check had been made out to the name I used as Makim's wife, and everyone at the restaurant knew me as Merinda Soldano.

Ron

I knew Merinda was serious about us, but I wasn't ready for a relationship like that, so I moved back to California. I had a lot of reasons: I wanted to go to Bible college. I wanted to know if this was true love. I had never known true love before. We talked to each other every day on the phone, I would go see her, and she would come see me.

She came to see me, too. One time, she showed up at the airport, turned around, lifted the back of her shirt, and said, "Look." She had "Ron" tattooed on her back. It really meant a lot to me. We conceived when she came to California that time. And on Father's Day, 2002, she told me she was pregnant. So, I moved back and became an instant father of twins.

I never tried to hide our relationship, and I don't think Merinda cared if Makim found out. One day she was at the computer with a few of the kids looking at my modeling pictures in an email, and Makim walked in and asked who that was. Merinda said: We're looking at Justin Timberlake look-alike pictures.

Makim said: That guy looks better than Justin Timberlake.

Moomoo was only two years old, and he said: That's Ron.

Makim threw the computer down the stairs and yelled at Merinda: Why would anyone like that want you?

He had her phones tapped; he had her followed. But we knew we were going for it.

Merinda's divorce was very bitter and ended poorly for her, but it left her free to remarry. So, we talked to Pastor Bob about getting married, and he showed us so much love, throughout it all. Something told him to marry us even though we had so much craziness going on in our lives. And he knew everything.

He knows everything about us and his family is very close to our hearts and our lives. He married us because he somehow knew we were meant for each other, even though it was an awkward time in both of our lives.

At our wedding, August 30, 2002, there was me and Merinda; Pastor Bob; my brothers, Michael and Raymond; the best man, Herb S.; and the guitar player, Jack. Merinda was the most gorgeous, gorgeous bride that I've ever seen.

Merinda and I believe that her story—this book—glorifies the name of Christ. We want to show who He is and what it means to be Christian. As a couple, we have been put together against all odds. Everybody I knew at the time said: No! Don't do it! You're making a huge mistake.

Christ ultimately is our first priority. Our marriage in the beginning was hell. In the beginning of our relationship, I saw what she had been through, and I vowed that I would love her past her pain. But then my own pain came up, and our marriage was a nightmare. I started to have my own troubles within myself. Becoming a father of six kids at 24 years old and having a wife that was so hurt, I began to have this anger build up inside of me. Then I started to become a guy who tried to take away all their pain, but that is a hard job to have. Only Christ can take away your pain.

One of the things that changed my life is what happened to Merinda when she was having the twins. It was about two weeks after the twins were born, and Merinda started losing a lot of blood in the bathroom. It was just gushing out of her. An ambulance came and took her directly to the Emergency Room. When we were waiting for her doctor to come, she started saying:

Please take care of the kids; promise me you will always be there for them.

I was like: Baby be quiet; what are you talking about?

Then she flat-lined. I kicked open the door and went to yell to the nurses but they were already on the run. I ran back in and screamed: NO!

I grabbed her shoulders and shook her. She opened her eyes and said: What, baby?

The machine restarted. Her doctor showed up to take her immediately back to surgery. Right before they pushed her stretcher through the huge double doors, I grabbed the doctor's arm with my left hand and spun him to look at me in the face. I stuck my right hand into his and said: Promise me you wont let her die.

He said: I promise.

They did an emergency hysterectomy on her, and she came out of the surgery having had an experience in heaven. When Merinda woke up in the recovery room, she was babbling about Maggie. She kept asking: Where's Maggie?

I said: You mean my mom? She's in California baby; we are in Memphis.

When she composed herself a little she said: I met Jesus, and your mom was there.

I didn't understand why my mother was there, because she is still alive. Pastor Bob explained that my mom represented the prayers that were immediately answered.

People can argue about the Bible and religion, but they can't take away something special like a second chance miracle, an experience with Christ. This marked a huge change in my life.

I was a screw-up before then. I'm not a knight on a white horse, but who I want to be is different now from who I used to be. I am so far from who I was when I met her. And this love we have is so different from the love I see in other couples. We care about what the other person thinks. When we're alone and it's just the two of us, we're straight-up with each other. I laugh about it sometimes, though because even if I didn't want to be totally honest with Merinda about everything, I have to, because she's got the gift of discerning spirit. There's no use in lying to her.

You can't watch "Law and Order" with her, either, or you'll just get mad. She always knows who did it. And don't try to pretend to be her friend if you have a hidden agenda, because she knows what is inside people. She has the gift of knowledge and wisdom. She's everything I ever wanted. I could not ask for more in a wife.

Merinda

THE DOCTOR TOLD ME NOT TO HAVE MORE KIDS, BUT I FELT RON should have a child of his own. On September 15, we went for ultrasound and the woman said: We're gonna be here for a while.

I got upset. I was worried about what was wrong. She said, "There are two heads." Ron almost passed out; he had this amazed look on his face. He was taking it all in: I'm going to be the father of twins. We could see that one was a boy and one was a girl.

Eight weeks before they were born, I started bleeding. They put me in the hospital and gave me shots. They didn't know if I was going to go into labor or not. I stayed there 26 days eating nothing but ice and popsicles. I was so hungry! Ron brought me three French fries because he wanted to help but he was so worried about whether that would help or hurt me. He went in the bathroom, took his hat off, and came back in the room with me. He was so young. He said: Should I meet my twins with my hat on or off?

He stayed by my side the whole time. He didn't go to sleep until about 4 a.m. that morning, and my water broke at at 7 a.m. I woke him up, and at 7:35 a.m. Ella was born. Then, a few moments later, Ronnie. I lost a lot of blood when they were being born. I was hemorrhaging so badly that I passed out.

When I came to, I was angry. I hadn't showered, I felt dirty and exhausted, and I had been through so much. An Indian doctor came in there and told me: The boy is fine, but the girl has Downs Syndrome. I ripped the needles out of my arm and demanded they take me to see my kids. Little Ronnie was on the right; Ella was on the left. Ronnie looked like all my other kids, but she did not. She had a head full of black hair, and she was so tiny, only four pounds. She was fine; she was not Downs Syndrome. But after we got home with them, she ran a fever, and we had to take her to Le Bonheur because that's where you take babies was under five pounds. Then they admitted me to St. Francis, because I was almost bleeding to death.

Ron was sitting beside me, and I said: Tell my kids I love them. I died that day. I don't know how long I was out—I was practically dead—but I saw Jesus. I came in contact with the biggest light, and I knew it was Jesus. And I saw Ron's mom. When I woke up from the surgery, I began to testify to Christ. And I asked Ron: Where's your mom? I had seen her; she was there when I was dying. The doctor told Ron that he couldn't believe I pulled through. He said: She fought for her life. But I was fighting for my children. God let me come back for a reason.

From 2005 to 2008, I worked in casinos in Tunica as a cocktail waitress. During that time, I also started working for a man who owned his own casino in Florida. He had charter flights to take older Italian and Jewish people to his casinos. I hosted his charter flights, flying with them from casino to casino, and he began to buy me presents. He never tried to have sex with me; he just bought me everything I wanted, including a car for my birthday.

That lifestyle led me to so many things that I'd never seen or done. I was hidden for so long. I never had a childhood; I had never had a teenage life at all. I had never gone to dances or done the things normal girls do. So, it was all very exciting to me, even though I was in my late twenties.

In the fall of '08, when the recession hit, Ron wanted us to move to Florida. He wanted to get away from the past that was haunting us in Memphis, and he thought his boss was going to give him work there.

Belal and Jahad, the older boys, were thirteen and seventeen, and Bessie was twenty and married and had a set of twins. The kids did not want to move, so I had to leave them there. Basically, we left Bessie with her twins and her two oldest brothers in our five-bedroom house. I started driving back and forth every other weekend. We lived in some moldy apartments in Panama City Beach. At first, we were making the mortgage payments but I couldn't find work right away and Ron didn't, either, so we couldn't make the payments. My older son started selling everything in it: the dining room table with a marble top and four chairs, the refrigerator, the microwave. I had no choice but to let the house go into foreclosure.

I had hardly ever had any liquor at that point in my life. But when I got off work at the casino, I would stay late and listen to the band, and I was getting free drinks there and as a hostess on the charter flights. I carried a gallon of vodka around with me like a baby, everywhere I went, even in front of my kids. I drank until I couldn't drink no more and went to bed with the vodka next to the bed. When I woke up, I took a shot. I think that I was so traumatized from all that had happened in my life, I was numb. But the drinking really didn't do anything. It didn't make me feel better; it didn't make me feel sad; I already felt sad. I felt that I had lost everything in my life by us moving away from my kids. I would go back and forth to Memphis all the time, seeing my kids and trying to get Jahad to come down to Florida. He was about thirteen and already six feet tall. I finally did get him to come visit for Christmas, and meanwhile we were having money troubles because of our work situations and our home life was terrible.

In the summer of 2011, we wanted to move back to Memphis. I didn't have a house to go to, but because of Ron, I had connections to the Church of the Harvest, and I knew they would help me. I wanted to get help for my drinking.

So he came with me and we moved into the home we live in now in Olive Branch, Mississippi. And the church helped us so much ever since we moved back: spiritually, financially, and psychologically.

I think I'm still caught up in some strongholds that are caught up in me and I want to let them go. I can go years without drinking and it doesn't bother me, but sometimes the devil gets to me and tells me that I need a drink. But I just need to do what the Lord needs me to do. Out of all this, what I've learned is that no matter what my dad did to me, or how much love my parents did or didn't show me—which wasn't much—was that I did give my children a better life than I had.

The other thing I understand now is that God is the only one that's going to be there for you. He's already done his work. He's waiting for us to follow along. He knows where we're going and where we want to be. He's waiting for us to get over the obstacles. He's like a navigator. He knows where you're going and where you need to be but isn't going to tell you there's a wrecked car in the way.

I think I'm still bound up in some strongholds that are tangled up inside me. I hope that telling my story in this book will help me release everything. I want to let it go. I try to let go. Sometimes, I think I have. But I get angry if somebody starts throwing things up in my face and blaming me. Ron says if I let it bother me then I haven't let it go.

There's a lot of love in this house. Ron and me pray every day before the kids go to school and at night before bed. I tried to be sure our kids knew they were loved, because I never got anything like that. It's so hard for little kids when they get taken the way I was, and set on a course that they didn't ask to be put on. It's a waste when a girl gets put in a position where she thinks she has nothing, she thinks she is nothing. It's a waste of a life when a girl thinks she has nobody in the world except the man who is bad to her, and people tell her: You'll never amount to anything. My prayers to the stars—if there is a God, get me out of here—were answered, and your prayers can be answered, too.

I've been degraded all my life. I survived a whole lot, starting with my childhood. I raised four kids myself, and then I found a man who loved me and I had two kids by him. Nobody can degrade me any more.

I want young women to understand that when you have a controlling boyfriend or husband and he beats you up and curses at you and calls you names to degrade who you are, that is not true. Don't believe it. Get away from it. Walk away. Don't live with that.

And I hope and pray to God that the Gypsy girls get ahold of this book, because I want them to know they don't have to quit school. No! They can have friends and make relationships throughout their life. They can go to the prom and do things with other kids. Stand up for yourself and move forward. Don't let the men in your life stop you from doing what you need to do. You can do anything you want to do in Christ Jesus. And that's what I've learned.

Ron and I help each other through each day. We could not do it without each other.

Because the biggest love comes through Jesus. You can't stop Jesus. I know that God has helped me through things nobody else could live through. God's always been there for me but I didn't know it. That's how it feels to me. I've never been perfect, but I've never forgotten Him. He is the only one that's going to be there for you. One thing I've learned from my pastor is that God has already done His work; He's waiting for us to follow along. He's waiting for us to get over the obstacles.

I don't feel that I am a good prayer. I am shy about praying. When we have the women's group at our church, sometimes a woman asks if I want to lead prayer. I always say: No. I don't think it would come out right if I prayed out loud. For a long time, I was embarrassed to even say: Amen. It was new to me. Now I do pray; I pray silently. I do my own certain prayers with my soul. I just want to live how the Lord wants me to live. I just want Him to talk to me. I try to listen, but I'm not perfect. I'm never going to be perfect, but I've never given up on God.

Made in the USA
Coppell, TX
29 December 2022